THE JOYS OF MOTHERHOOD

by
Barbara & Jim Dale

Andrews and McMeel
A Universal Press Syndicate Company
Kansas City

ISBN: 0-8362-3047-7

Library of Congress Catalog #: 93-73440

Now we have children. Little miniature humans who rely on us to be responsible and level-headed and all those other things our mothers kept telling us we weren't.

Children!!! You can't return them or put them on layaway. This is strictly all sales final.

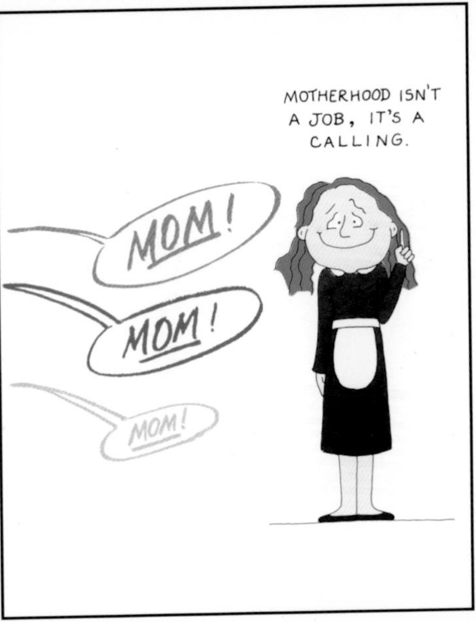
MOM!
MOM!
MOM!
MOTHERHOOD ISN'T A JOB, IT'S A CALLING.

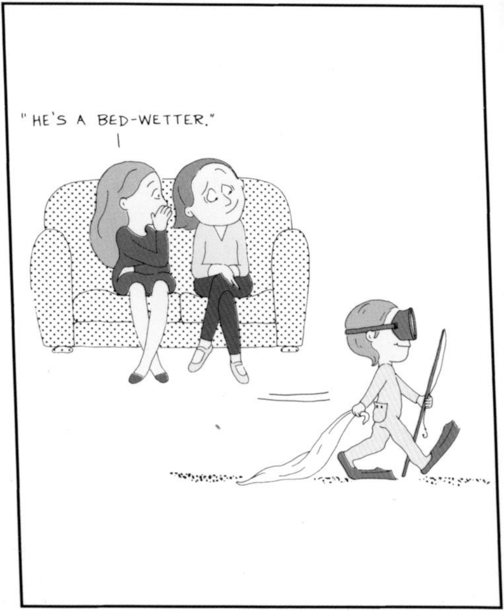
"HE'S A BED-WETTER."

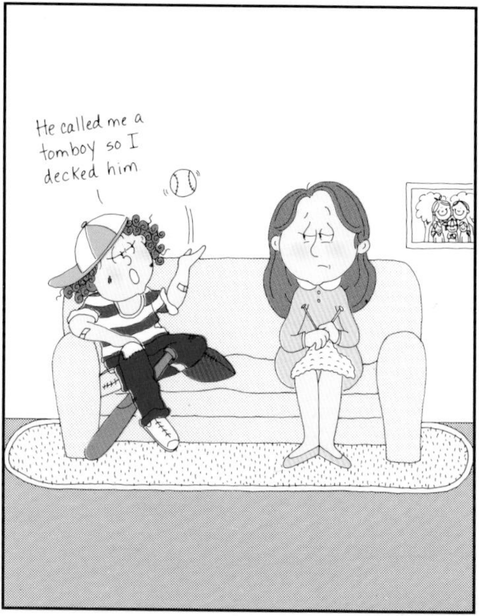
He called me a tomboy so I decked him

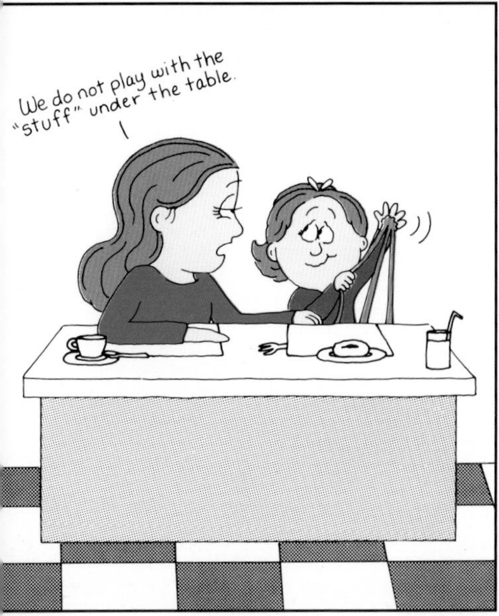
We do not play with the "stuff" under the table.

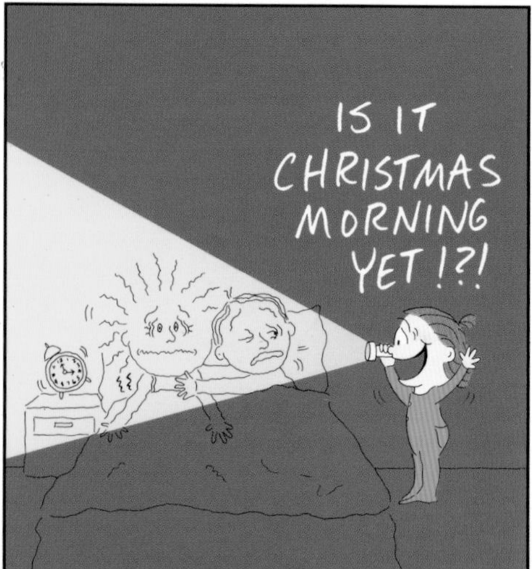
IS IT CHRISTMAS MORNING YET !?!

...AND THIS IS A PICTURE OF MOMMY BEFORE SHE HAD A BABY, BACK WHEN SHE WAS WILLING TO BE SEEN IN PUBLIC IN A BATHING SUIT...

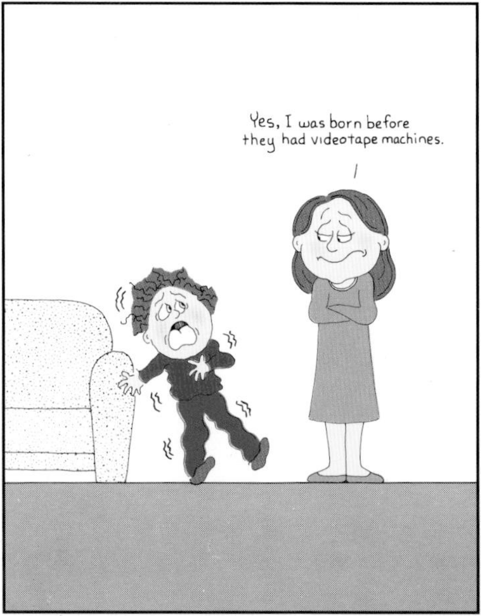
Yes, I was born before they had videotape machines.

"I THINK I'M FINALLY BEGINNING
TO UNDERSTAND YOUR DECISION."

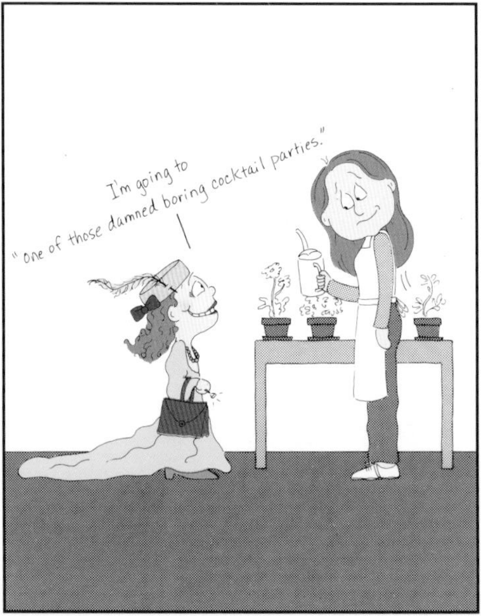
I'm going to
"one of those damned boring cocktail parties."

This is a simple arrangement just between us.
You get the cake and you never, <u>repeat</u> <u>never</u>,
reveal the number you saw when Mommy
was on the bathroom scale.

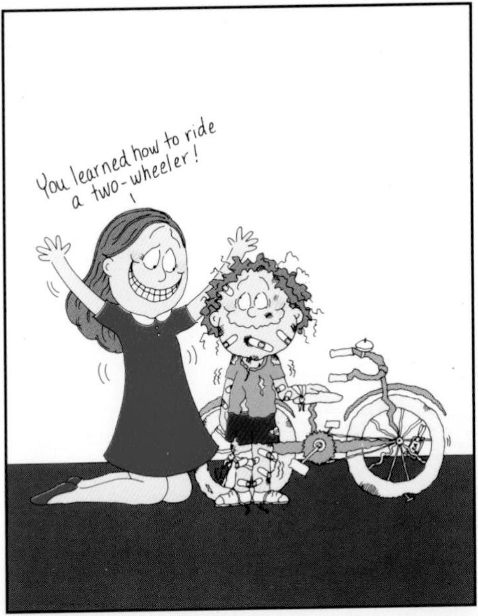
You learned how to ride a two-wheeler!

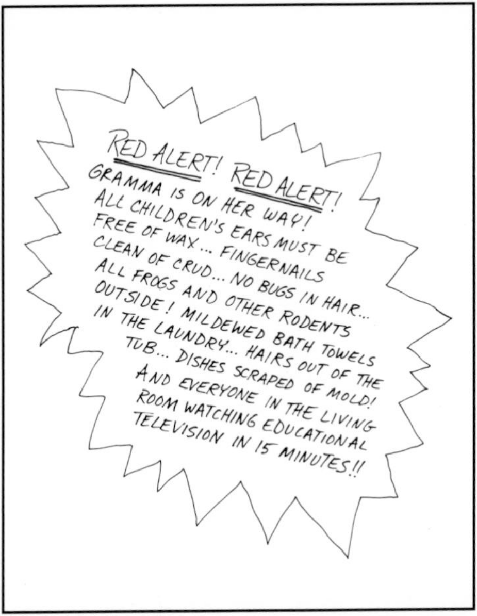
RED ALERT! RED ALERT!
GRAMMA IS ON HER WAY!
ALL CHILDREN'S EARS MUST BE FREE OF WAX... FINGERNAILS CLEAN OF CRUD... NO BUGS IN HAIR... ALL FROGS AND OTHER RODENTS OUTSIDE! MILDEWED BATH TOWELS IN THE LAUNDRY... HAIRS OUT OF THE TUB... DISHES SCRAPED OF MOLD!
AND EVERYONE IN THE LIVING ROOM WATCHING EDUCATIONAL TELEVISION IN 15 MINUTES!!

These "yucky-icky" ones
Mommy will eat for
you because she
loves you.

Even though you say you hate your sister, you really love your sister because she's your sister and it just SEEMS like you hate her and you really WOULD hate her if she WASN'T your sister, but since she IS, you DON'T. Understand?

The kids are really looking forward to you sitting this Saturday, Angela.

I DON'T LIKE YOU TO TALK TO
ME LIKE THAT.

I DON'T LIKE YOU TO LEAVE
YOUR ROOM SUCH A MESS.

I DON'T LIKE YOUR FRIENDS
HANGING AROUND ALL DAY.

AND I ESPECIALLY DON'T
LIKE THE FACT THAT YOU'RE
TALLER THAN ME.

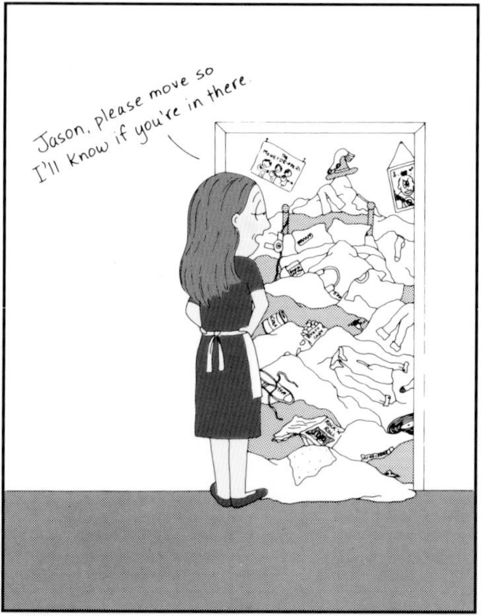
Jason, please move so
I'll know if you're in there.

I WILL NOT COME OUT FOR DINNER. I WILL NOT COME OUT AT ALL TONIGHT... OR TOMORROW NIGHT... OR FOR MY BIRTHDAY... OR GRADUATION... OR EVER AGAIN IN MY LIFE!!!
KEEP OUT!

When they cross the stage and take that diploma I'll be fine. I'll just take a deep breath, close my eyes, make a mental picture of this wonderful moment . . . and weep uncontrollably for thirty or forty straight hours.

My baby's gone!!!!

Just when I was getting good at this mother stuff.

But, on the other hand, it does free up a whole room of the house.